WEARING A BLINDFOLD, IDENTIFY THREE OBJECTS USING JUST YOUR TONGUE.

I DARE YOU TO

I DARE YOU TO

Improvise a rap about a person in your group.

I DARE YOU TO

Bite into a lemon or a raw onion – it's your choice, but you must chew and swallow at least one mouthful.

I DARE YOU TO

Allow someone to draw whatever they like on your face (or backside) in semi-permanent marker.

I DARE YOU TO

Swap phones with someone and...

... send a suggestive message to each other's partner or crush. 😄😄😄😄

I DARE YOU TO

I DARE YOU TO

DO A SEXY DANCE FOR SOMEONE WHILE STANDING ON ONE LEG.

I DARE YOU TO

PRETEND TO AUCTION OFF ANOTHER PLAYER BASED ON THEIR POTENTIAL AS A ROMANTIC PARTNER.

I DARE YOU TO

I DARE YOU TO

I DARE YOU TO

DO YOUR BEST IMPERSONATION OF THE PERSON TO YOUR LEFT.

I DARE YOU TO

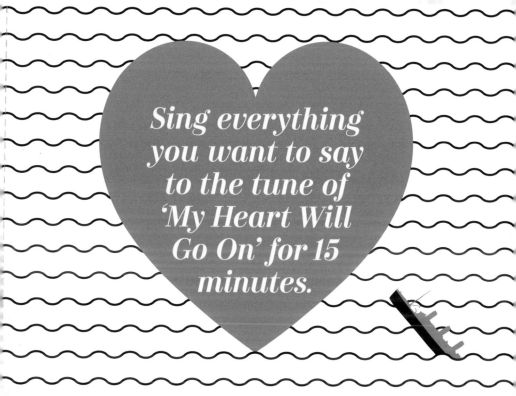

Sing everything you want to say to the tune of 'My Heart Will Go On' for 15 minutes.

I DARE YOU TO

Acquire a condom,

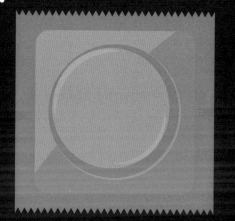

but not from a *shop* or a *machine*.

I DARE YOU TO

START A CONGA LINE, WHEREVER YOU ARE, AND GET TOTAL STRANGERS TO JOIN IN.

I DARE YOU TO

Communicate only through interpretive dance for one hour.

I DARE YOU TO

WALK SIDEWAYS LIKE A CRAB FOR THE NEXT HOUR.

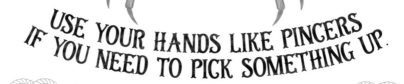

USE YOUR HANDS LIKE PINCERS IF YOU NEED TO PICK SOMETHING UP.

I DARE YOU TO

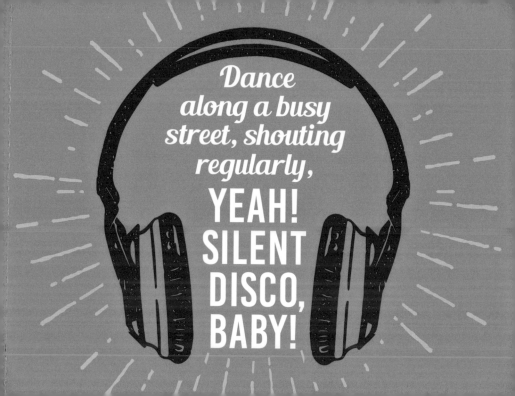

I DARE YOU TO

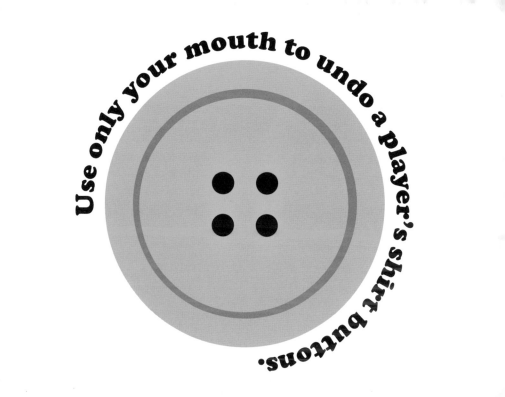

Use only your mouth to undo a player's shirt buttons.

I DARE YOU TO

I DARE YOU TO

Take pictures of yourself imitating emojis and send three to a friend without any explanation.

I DARE YOU TO

I DARE YOU TO

I DARE YOU TO

I DARE YOU TO

I DARE YOU TO

PRETEND YOU'RE A CHICKEN AND PECK AT SOME BREAKFAST CEREAL SCATTERED ON THE FLOOR.

I DARE YOU TO